The Bikepacking Bible

THE BIKEPACKING BIBLE

The Practical Guide to Self-Supported Adventure Cycling

RICHARD A. PERRY

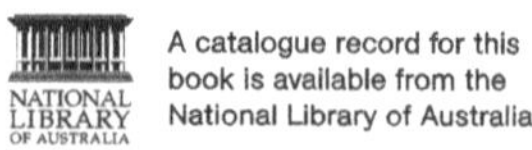

A catalogue record for this book is available from the National Library of Australia

*For every rider who has ever wondered what was beyond
the next hill - and had the courage to find out.*

Contents

Introduction

Why Bikepacking Changes People

There is a moment, usually somewhere far from traffic noise and mobile reception, when bikepacking stops being a trip and becomes something else entirely.

It might happen on a long gravel climb when your legs are burning and the only sound is wind moving through trees.

It might happen when you unzip your tent at sunrise and realise you slept somewhere most people will never see.

Or it might happen when you fix a mechanical problem alone, miles from help, and realise you are far more capable than you thought.

Bikepacking is not just cycling.
It is not just camping.
And it is definitely not just another outdoor hobby.

Bikepacking is independence.

At its core, bikepacking strips life back to essentials. You carry what you need. You move using your own power. You solve problems as they appear. And somewhere along the way, the noise of modern life fades into the background.

This book exists for one simple reason: to help you do this safely, confidently, and enjoyably.

Not everyone has years of outdoor experience. Not everyone grew up camping or riding bikes long distances. And that's okay. Bikepacking is one of the most accessible forms of adventure travel in the world, as long as you approach it with preparation, knowledge, and respect for the environments you travel through.

Inside this book, you will not find unrealistic expedition stories or gear lists designed for professional explorers. Instead, you will find practical, tested advice designed for real people with real lives - people who want to explore further than day rides but don't know where to begin.

You will learn:

- 🚲 How to choose the right bike without wasting money
- 🚲 What gear actually matters (and what doesn't)
- 🚲 How to plan routes that are challenging but achievable
- 🚲 How to stay safe when things go wrong
- 🚲 How to build confidence trip by trip

You will also learn something else, something most guides don't talk about enough.

Bikepacking changes how you see yourself.

When you carry your life on a bike and move across landscapes under your own power, you stop thinking of yourself as someone who "goes riding" and start thinking of yourself as someone who can go anywhere.

That shift matters.

This book is written as if we're sitting together after a ride, having an honest conversation about what works, what doesn't, and what I wish someone had told me when I first started.

In each chapter, you'll find a straight-talking section that makes it clear what needs to be addressed and what can safely be ignored. You'll also discover Pro Tips to help sharpen your skills, Real-World Examples that bring key points to life, and some of my personal Tales from the Trails - stories that show the kinds of great experiences you can build along the way.

If you are new to bikepacking, this book will give you a clear, safe path forward.

If you already ride and want to go further, this book will help you refine your systems and make trips more efficient and enjoyable.

If you are dreaming about a big adventure one day, this book will help you realise that you don't have to wait. You can start building towards it right now.

The only thing you really need to begin is curiosity - and the willingness to keep pedalling when things get hard.

CHAPTER 1

What Bikepacking Really Is
(And What It Isn't)

If you search online for bikepacking, you will see photos of remote mountain ranges, desert crossings, and riders covered in dust, smiling next to heavily loaded bikes.

Those images are inspiring, but they can also be misleading.

Bikepacking is not about suffering.
It is not about being the toughest rider.
And it is definitely not about how your trip looks on social media.

Bikepacking is simply self-supported travel by bicycle, usually over mixed terrain, using lightweight gear systems designed to keep the bike rideable on rough surfaces.

That definition matters, because it removes intimidation.

You do not need to cross continents to be a bikepacker.
You do not need expensive gear.
You do not need elite fitness.

Your first bikepacking trip might be:

- 🚴 One night in a local national park
- 🚴 A weekend gravel loop
- 🚴 A rail trail ride with camping at the end

And that counts.

Different types of cycling

Traditional **touring cycling** usually involves:

- 🚲 Panniers mounted on racks
- 🚲 Heavier loads
- 🚲 Mostly road-based travel
- 🚲 Town-to-town resupply options

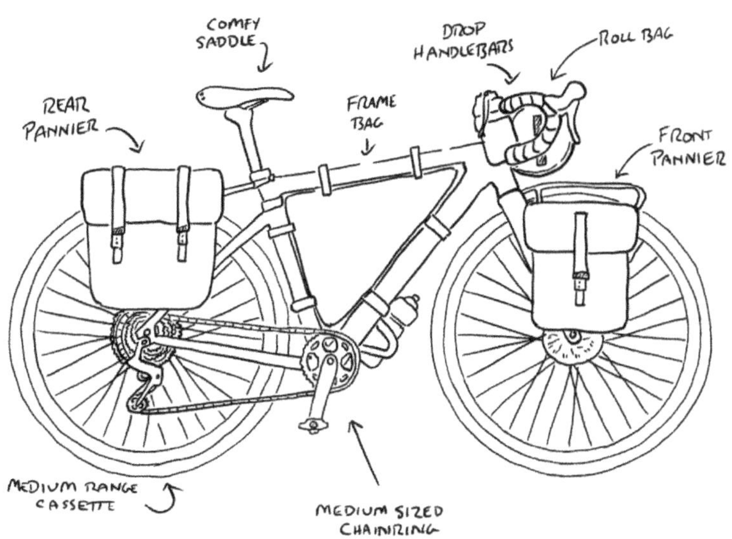

Road cycling usually involves:

- Lightest possible set up
- A banana for lunch
- Speed more important than comfort
- Aero designs

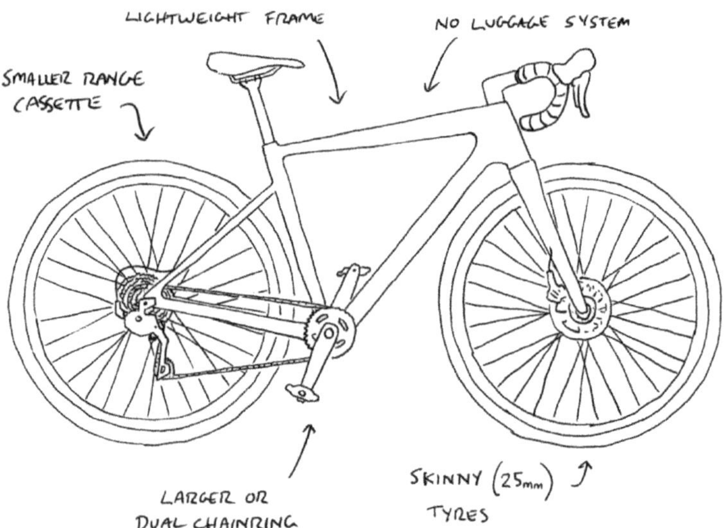

Mountain biking usually involves:

- Different frame style
- Suspension
- Climbing capability more import than speed
- Wide knobbly tyres

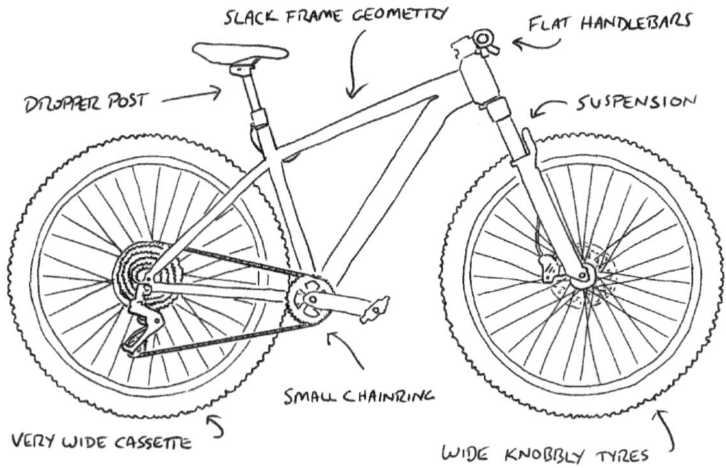

Bikepacking usually involves:

- 🚲 Frame bags, saddle bags, and handlebar rolls
- 🚲 Lighter overall weight than a touring bike
- 🚲 Off-road or mixed terrain routes
- 🚲 Greater self-sufficiency than road / MTB bikes

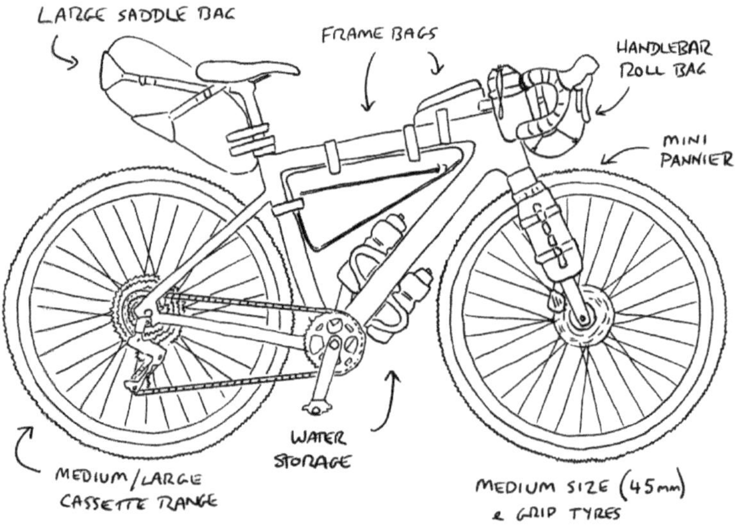

None of these options are better than the other. They are simply different tools for different styles of travel.

Bikepacking excels when:

- 🚲 Terrain is rough or remote
- 🚲 You want to travel lighter
- 🚲 You want to explore trails, fire roads, or backcountry routes

The Three Pillars of Bikepacking

Over time, most successful bikepackers learn the same core lessons. Everything comes back to three pillars.

1. Efficiency

Every item you carry has a cost. Weight affects climbing, fatigue, bike handling, and enjoyment.

2. Self-Reliance

You must be able to solve problems without immediate help. This includes navigation, basic repairs, and risk assessment.

3. Adaptability

Weather changes. Routes change. Your body changes. The ability to adjust plans is more important than sticking to them perfectly.

The Biggest Myth: "I'm Not Ready Yet"

Most people delay bikepacking because they think they need:

 Better fitness

Better gear

More experience

The truth is the opposite.

You gain fitness by riding.
You understand gear by using it.
You gain experience by starting small and building up.

The safest and smartest way to become a bikepacker is not by waiting until you feel ready - it is by taking manageable steps forward.

The Real Goal

The goal of bikepacking is not distance.

The goal is freedom.

Freedom to choose your route.
Freedom to move at your own pace.
Freedom to experience landscapes in a way cars and planes never allow.

The core of bikepacking is the ability to travel for as far as you want, for as long as you want, with the minimal amount of effort, gear, and support.

Greater distance and difficulty can come later, if you want them to.

But the real reward is something much simpler: learning that you are capable of more than you thought.

And that lesson rarely stays on the trail. It tends to follow you back into the rest of your life.

To achieve these goals, it may be that you need to compromise and tailor your set up to best suit you. Bikepacking is a constant trade-off between efficiency and comfort. The right selection for you will depend on your abilities, the tracks you will be riding on, how much luggage you need, and also how fast you want to go. We will review this in more depth later on, including pro tips on how to build the right bike for you.

 *Tales from the trails...*

Jake.

I met him somewhere in US, where the horizons are wide, the wind has opinions, and every cyclist looks slightly ragged.

He was riding what could generously be described as a "well-loved" steel bike. It had clearly seen things. The paint was tired, the drivetrain sounded philosophical, and the collection of bags attached to it appeared to have been assembled through a combination of straps, cord, optimism, and mild defiance of physics.

His cycling shoes were a pair of brown Crocs. They may have been white once, it was hard to tell.

His kickstand? A carefully whittled hickory stick, which he produced with quiet pride each time he parked. It worked flawlessly.

I'm fairly certain his entire setup - bike, bags, clothing, sleep system, cooking kit, everything - cost less than a modern smartphone.

And yet Jake was one of the happiest, most content cyclists I've ever met.

He'd been on the road for a couple of years, meandering across the United States in wide, joyful zigzags - north to south, east to west, and frequently in directions that didn't appear on maps. He wasn't chasing segments, records, or gear upgrades. He was simply riding.

There was one particularly memorable moment involving Jake and Tony, his riding buddy for the day, and a pair of very well-equipped riders.

They first rolled up alongside Tony, one of them offered, in what I'm sure was intended as helpful sincerity, "You might want to think about putting some wider tyres on that."

They then drifted forward and pulled alongside Jake himself, something interesting happened.

Silence.

Not awkward silence. Not hostile silence. Just the quiet, dawning realisation that they had absolutely no idea where to begin unpacking what they were looking at.

Jake, and his Crocs, continued pedalling with complete serenity.

The wider tyres conversation not repeated.

There was no anxiety in Jake. No comparison. No performance.

Just movement.

It's easy to believe adventure requires perfect equipment. Jake is living proof that it doesn't.

Good on you Jake, you are amazing!

CHAPTER 2

Why People Become Bikepackers

Most people don't wake up one morning and decide to become bikepackers.

Usually, it starts smaller than that.

Maybe you enjoy riding but feel limited by day rides. Maybe you like camping but want a more active way to explore. Maybe you are looking for something that feels like an adventure without needing months off work or huge financial investment.

Bikepacking sits in a rare space between accessibility and adventure. It offers experiences that feel big and meaningful, without requiring you to be an elite athlete or professional explorer.

Over time, I've noticed most riders arrive at bikepacking through one of six motivations.

1. The Search for Simplicity

Modern life is loud. Notifications, schedules, expectations, and constant information can make it feel like your brain never fully switches off.

Bikepacking forces brutal simplicity.

Your world becomes:

- Where is water?
- Where will I sleep?
- Wow, what a view!
- How far can I comfortably ride today?
- What is the weather doing?

And that's it.

That level of simplicity is surprisingly powerful. Many riders describe their first multi-day trip as mentally calming in a way they didn't expect.

 **Real-World Example**

On a three-day gravel loop through regional farmland, a rider I met at a campsite told me something that stuck with me. He said the best part of the trip wasn't the scenery - it was that nobody needed anything from him for the last few days. No emails. No meetings. No deadlines.

Just riding, eating, setting up camp, and sleeping.

That reset is a huge part of why people come back to bikepacking again and again.

2. The Desire for Real Adventure

Adventure doesn't have to mean danger or extreme risk. Real adventure simply means uncertainty + challenge.

Bikepacking gives you:

- Changing terrain
- Changing weather
- Real physical effort
- Problem-solving moments

Even small trips feel meaningful because you are fully responsible for the outcome.

3. Physical Challenge with Purpose

Training rides are great. But riding with a destination changes everything.

When you know you need to reach the next water source or campsite, effort becomes meaningful. Many riders find they can ride further and push harder when the ride has purpose.

4. Connection to Landscape

Cars isolate you from environments. Hiking limits how far you can realistically travel.

Bikepacking sits in a perfect middle ground:

- 🚲 Fast enough to cover real distance
- 🚲 Slow enough to be immersed in the landscape

You feel temperature changes, smell forests, notice terrain shifts, hear your tyres rumbling on the gravel. You get to understand landscapes in a deeper way.

5. Build Amazing Relationships

Bikepacking causes you to think differently about people, the remoteness triggers a survival instinct that drives you to connect with the few people around you to a deeper level.

- 🚲 Long term mates become closer than family
- 🚲 People you meet for the first time become lifelong friends

🚲 You engage strangers like you have known them for years

Riders will often say that they also get to meet themselves, being alone with you own thoughts for days on end is a great way to answer the questions that you have been meaning to ask yourself for years.

6. The Confidence Effect

Bikepacking quietly builds confidence.

You learn you can:

🚲 Navigate unfamiliar places
🚲 Solve problems under pressure
🚲 Manage your energy and resources
🚲 Stay calm when things don't go to plan

That confidence transfers into everyday life.

CHAPTER 3

Preparing for Your First Adventure

The biggest mistake beginners make is assuming preparation means buying gear.

Preparation actually means reducing unknowns.

Buying more gear will slow you down, doing more preparation will keep you going no matter what changes.

Your first goal is not to be fast.
It is not to be impressive.
It is not to be extreme.

Your first goal is to have a trip where nothing surprises you in a dangerous way.

Step 1: Start Smaller Than You Think You Need To

Your first trip should feel almost too easy.

Ideal first trip:

-  1 night
- Known terrain
- Multiple exit options
- Reliable weather window
- Easy water access

 **Real-World Example**

A rider I coached once planned a 4-day remote trip as their first bikepacking experience. We scaled it back to one overnight loop. On that trip, he discovered:

- *His saddle was uncomfortable after 4 hours*
- *His sleep system was too cold*
- *He packed twice as much food as needed*

Fixing those things on a short trip prevented a miserable long trip later.

Step 2: Test Gear Before You Trust It

Never use untested gear on a remote trip.

Test:

- Sleep system in backyard or local camp
- Stove system multiple times
- Packing setup on long day rides
- Navigation tools without mobile signal

Step 3: Route Planning Basics

Good beginner routes include:

- Rail trails
- Fire roads
- National Park management roads
- Gravel touring routes

Avoid early on:

- Technical mountain bike trails
- Long waterless sections
- Highly remote desert routes
- High alpine weather exposure

Step 4: Tell Someone Your Plan

Always share:

- Route map
- Start and finish times
- Emergency contact plan

This is not optional in remote riding.

> **⚡ PRO TIP**
>
> Once you have a few shorter rides under your belt, develop and follow a training plan for longer more demanding adventures.

A 3-month training plan is more than enough for a 1-week adventure.

The first month of the training plan should concentrate on increasingly frequent shorter distance rides to get you used to riding day after day.

The second month should stretch the distances in these rides so you can stay in the saddle for longer and further.

The last month should get you closer to the daily distances you intend to be riding on your adventure, as frequently as you can.

This will reduce the shock to your system in transitioning from weekend rides to a longer adventure.

In Chapter 15 there is a different plan to prepare you for a multi-week ride.

The Classic Rookie Error - Overpacking

What Riders Often Wish They'd Left at Home...

One of the quiet rites of passage in bikepacking is finishing a trip and realising you carried things you never once used.

It happens to almost everyone.

Overpacking rarely comes from carelessness - it usually comes from uncertainty. When you're not yet sure what a trip will demand, it feels safer to prepare for every possible scenario. The result is often a bike that feels heavier than it needs to be, and a rider working harder than necessary.

Here are some of the most common items people later realise they didn't truly need.

Too Many Clothes

It's natural to imagine wanting fresh options each day. Extra jerseys, spare trousers, backup layers "just in case."

In practice, most riders rotate a small core kit. A riding outfit, something comfortable for camp, and weather protection are usually enough. Clothing is one of the fastest ways to add weight without noticing it.

With experience, you begin to trust that re-wearing gear is simply part of the rhythm.

Large Comfort Items

Comfort matters. It genuinely does.

But there's a difference between thoughtful comfort and bulky reassurance. Camp chairs, large pillows, or full-size towels often seem appealing at home. After a long climb, they can feel like unnecessary ballast.

Small, lightweight versions usually provide most of the benefit without the burden.

More Food Than Necessary

Early trips often include a surplus of snacks and emergency meals. Food feels like security.

Yet most routes pass through villages, shops, or cafés more often than we imagine. Carrying reasonable margins is wise; carrying several days of surplus "just in case" can turn into avoidable weight.

Learning your true daily intake takes experience. That understanding is built ride by ride.

Extra Tools and Spares

There's reassurance in being mechanically prepared. But bringing tools you don't know how to use - or duplicates of the same tool - rarely adds real safety.

A focused repair kit tailored to your specific bike is almost always enough. Confidence comes more from familiarity than quantity.

Full-Size Toiletries

It's surprising how quickly small, everyday items add up. A large sunscreen bottle or full toothpaste tube may not seem significant on its own, but collectively they contribute to weight and bulk.

Decanting essentials into smaller containers is a small change that makes a noticeable difference.

"Just in Case" Electronics

Tablets, multiple cameras, extra batteries, speakers - they all promise enjoyment. Some riders truly use them. Many discover they're too tired in the evenings to do much more than eat and rest.

If a device supports navigation, safety, or something deeply meaningful to you, it earns its place. If it's simply there to ease uncertainty, or in case you get bored - leave it at home.

The Things We Pack for Anxiety

This is the quiet category that doesn't appear on packing lists.

Sometimes we carry items not because we will use them, but because leaving them behind feels uncomfortable. The more experience you gain, the more you recognise that preparation isn't about carrying everything - it's about carrying what genuinely serves you.

 ## *Tales from the trails...*

After a long, sun-soaked day of dust, sweat, and quiet questioning of our life choices, my riding mate and I rolled into a ranger station reasonably grim faced. And there it was: water. Glorious, flowing, civilisation-flavoured water.

We parked ourselves under the nearest tree and began the ritual of boiling some water for our dehydrated sawdust with beef.

Not long after, another group arrived. They looked... seasoned. Not in the competent way - more in the slow-roasted way. They too were thrilled by the unexpected water source.

Then they began unpacking.

First came the mini camp chairs. Fair enough. Then a steel BBQ emerged. A full-size SLR camera followed. And finally - a ukulele.

We tried not to stare. We failed.

"Luxury items," one of them explained.

As the conversation unfolded, it became clear that these "luxuries" had slowly transformed into travelling regrets. The BBQ hadn't been lit once. The ukulele had not improved morale. The chairs had mostly served as symbolic reminders of poor judgement.

They confided that the entire collection was destined to be despatched back home at the first post office they encountered.

We wished them luck, and quietly, we then reviewed our own bags.

Use early short rides to hone your packing skills

Almost every rider overpacks on their first trip. Many overpack on their second. That isn't a mistake; it's part of the learning process.

Each journey teaches you what truly matters.

The aim isn't extreme minimalism. It's thoughtful efficiency - carrying enough to feel safe and comfortable, but not so much that the weight steals energy from the ride itself.

Over time, your packing becomes simpler. And as it does, the ride feels lighter - not just physically, but mentally as well.

That's when you begin to feel truly free.

CHAPTER 4

Choosing the Right Bike (Without Wasting Money)

The best bikepacking bike is the one you already own - if it is safe and suitable for the terrain you plan to ride.

Marketing can make it seem like you need a specialised bikepacking bike. Most riders don't. After you have been bikepacking for a while you will have seen all types of bikes on all types of trails.

Sooner or later, things will wear out, and you will be more experienced. This is the time to refine your bike and gear. Chapter 17 explains this in detail. It's at the back of the book for a reason.

The Three Most Common Bikepacking Platforms

Gravel Bikes

Best for:

- Mixed road and gravel
- Long distance efficiency (speed vs. effort)
- Lighter gear setups

Limitations:

- Less comfortable on rough trails
- Limited tyre width (model dependent) meaning limited stability in loose surfaces

Hardtail Mountain Bikes

Best for:

- Rough / steep terrain
- Technical trails
- Comfort over long off-road days

Limitations:

- Slower on sealed roads
- Slightly heavier overall
- Additional complexity brings increased failure points
- Limited luggage capacity

Adventure / Touring Bikes

Best for:

- Stability under load
- Long-distance mixed terrain
- Riders who prefer durability over speed

Limitations:

- Slower everywhere
- Heaviest option
- Unable to tackle technical terrain

Fit Matters More Than Bike Type

Comfort prevents injuries and fatigue.

Focus on:

- Saddle comfort
- Reach and posture
- Hand positions
- Pedal efficiency
- Vibrations and dampening
- Simple dependable components

 **Real-World Example**

One experienced rider I met completed a 2,000 km trip on a 10-year-old aluminium hardtail. Not because it was perfect - but because it fitted well and was self-serviceable.

Reliability beats perfection every time.

Evolving your set up

If you feel nervous on loose / sandy / soft terrain, then lower your tyre pressures, or max-out the size of tyre you can fit in your frame.

If you get pins and needles in your feet after a few hours, then switch to large flat pedals and simple walking shoes instead of bike shoes and cleats.

If your hands and wrists are getting fatigued with vibrations, fit a shock absorbing stem (e.g. Redshift).

Doing these lower cost changes will help you evolve your set up gradually over time. It reveals what issues concern you the most and highlighting solid tactics to resolve them.

This knowledge and experience will drive bigger decisions later on.

CHAPTER 5

Gear Systems
That Actually Work

Gear is one of the biggest barriers to entry in bikepacking - mostly because people think they need perfect gear before they can start.

You don't.

You need **reliable gear**, not perfect gear.

The best bikepackers aren't the ones with the newest equipment. They're the ones who understand how their gear works, what it can handle, and where its limits are.

Think of gear as tools. Tools don't need to be impressive - they need to be dependable and useful.

If there is one mindset shift that will make your bikepacking life easier, it is this:

You are building a system, not collecting products.

The Core Gear System Philosophy

Every item you carry should do at least one of three things:

1.   Keep you safe
2.   Keep you moving
3.   Help you recover for the next day

If it doesn't do at least one of those things, it doesn't need to be in your kit. This is incredibly freeing once you accept it.

The Five Core Gear Categories

You can simplify all bikepacking gear into five core systems:

1. Shelter System

This includes:

- Tent / bivvy / tarp / hammock
- Groundsheet (if needed)
- Pegs and guy lines

Your shelter's job is simple: protect you from weather and allow quality sleep.

Modern bikepacking tents are ultralight, have short poles, pack down small.

A bivvy is the smallest system to keep you out of the weather but can be difficult to wriggle in/out of.

A tarp is only really useful to keep the rain off, and potentially the wind if you can rig it up well.

Hammocks are suitable for warm / dry climates, but can be difficult to sleep comfortably in, and are reliant on you being in a forest.

2. Sleep System

This includes:

- Sleeping bag or quilt
- Sleeping mat or pad (or both)
- Pillow (optional but morale-boosting)

Sleep is not luxury. Sleep is performance recovery.

If you are slightly too warm, then you are in the right sleeping system, if you are cold, you are not.

3. Clothing System

This includes:

- Riding clothing
- Camp clothing
- Weather protection layers

Your clothing system regulates temperature, moisture, and comfort.

4. Nutrition and Hydration System

This includes:

- Food storage
- Cooking system (if used)
- Water storage and filtration

Food keeps you moving. Water keeps you alive.

5. Repair and Safety System

This includes:

- Tools
- Spares
- First aid
- Navigation
- Emergency communication

This is your independence system.

 **Real-World Example**

On a windy ridge ride, I once watched a rider unpack three different comfort items - but they didn't have a waterproof shell. When the weather turned, they had to stop riding early.

Comfort gear is great.
Survival gear is essential.

Build your essential system first, then see if you have any space left.

The Biggest Gear Mistake: Packing FOMO (fear of missing out)

As mentioned before, new bikepackers often pack "just in case" items for every possible scenario.

The problem is that every extra item costs energy.

Weight is cumulative fatigue.

A good rule:
If you are packing items for a scenario that has less than a 5% chance of happening - and it isn't life-threatening - leave it at home.

 *Tales from the trails...*

There is one final subject I have to raise - slightly awkward, deeply important, and entirely capable of ending your adventure early if neglected.

It doesn't neatly fit into packing systems, nutrition plans, or mechanical preparation. It is, in many ways, its own ecosystem.

Your backside.

More specifically, the delicate and ongoing relationship between your backside, your saddle, and the diplomatic mediator known as your cycling shorts.

If that relationship deteriorates, everything else becomes irrelevant.

You can have perfect gearing, flawless navigation, and stunning scenery - but if sitting down feels like lowering yourself onto a collection of bad decisions, morale collapses quickly.

I have seen a wide range of coping strategies.

Some riders double up on padded shorts, effectively building a foam-based suspension system. Others apply chamois cream with the kind of generosity normally reserved for icing a cake - occasionally opting for formulas that include mild local anaesthetic, which feels innovative until you realise numbness is not always a long-term solution.

And, unfortunately, I have known strong, fit riders who have had to end trips early because the situation became unmanageable.

The truth is simple: this relationship needs time.

You cannot rush it. You cannot negotiate it mid-expedition.

Your saddle, shorts, and skin need weeks of shared miles to reach a place of quiet trust. Small discomforts in training should not be ignored - they are warnings.

When the relationship works, you barely think about it.

When it doesn't, you think about nothing else.

Build that trust early. Your future self - somewhere on Day Nine, climbing gently into the cloud base - will be profoundly grateful.

CHAPTER 6

Packing Like a Professional

Packing is not about fitting everything onto your bike.

Packing is about **protecting ride quality**.

A poorly packed bike feels unstable, inefficient, and exhausting to ride.

A well-packed bike feels surprisingly normal - even fully loaded.

The Three Zone Packing Rule

Zone 1 - Core Frame Area

Best for:

- Heavy / dense items
- Water
- Tools

This keeps weight low and centred.

Zone 2 - Handlebar Area

Best for:

- Light bulky items
- Sleeping gear
- Clothing layers

Avoid putting heavy or dense items here - it affects steering, stability and bike responsiveness.

Zone 3 - Saddle Area

Best for:

- Medium weight soft gear
- Clothing
- Sleep layers
- Camp gear

Avoid heavy items - it affects bike handling.

 *Real-World Example*

On a multi-day gravel ride, a rider packed all water in a saddle bag. The bike felt unstable descending. After moving water into frame storage, bike control improved immediately.

Weight placement matters as much as total weight.

Packing Mindset: Pack for Access, Not Just Space

Ask:

What do I need quickly during the day?

Usually:

 Snacks

 Rain jacket

 Navigation device

 Sunscreen

 Phone

These should be easy to reach without unpacking your whole bike.

The 80% Packing Rule

If your bags are 100% full before you leave, you have packed too much.

Leave 20% space for:

- 🚴 Food resupply
- 🚴 Layer changes
- 🚴 Small purchases
- 🚴 Unexpected needs

 ## Tales from the trails...

With grand, heroic intentions of crossing vast remote stretches where the water tasted faintly of sulphur and bad decisions, I decided to set my bike up like a fully loaded expedition tourer. Front panniers. Rear panniers. Enough water and food to survive minor civilisation collapse.

The logic was flawless. The execution… less so.

About 10km into the ride, we rolled into a sweeping descent.

Then my bike began to wobble.

Not a gentle wiggle. A full, high-speed shimmy. Anything over 20kmh and the handlebars developed opinions of their own. I found myself gripping them like a competitive arm wrestler, trying to negotiate peace between gravity and poor packing strategy.

Meanwhile, my riding partner descended gracefully, like a well-balanced gazelle. I still cannot forget his penetrating stare.

For the next few days, I shifted water bottles, moved food bags, redistributed gear and improved things. I reduced the wobble from "terrifying" to "mildly concerning."

But I never fully eliminated it.

I should have tested this setup before departure.

Not half-loaded.

Not "roughly about right."

But full weight. Full water. Full food.

The trail is an honest teacher. It doesn't mind if your packing plan looked excellent on paper.

Graham was not fast. I'm not entirely convinced he used the smaller half of his cassette. But he was relentless.

One afternoon we noticed he was limping.

"What happened?" we asked.

"Oh, I lost a sandal a few days ago," he replied casually. "So I just walk with one now. Sometimes I swap feet if it gets too sore."

No drama. No complaint. Just rotational sandal management.

A couple of days later, we passed a service station. I bought him a new pair of flip-flops. When we handed them over that evening, he reacted as though we'd presented him with a winning lottery ticket and a puppy.

Pure joy.

The moral?

Pack the right gear. And once you do - try not to scatter it across the trail you are on.

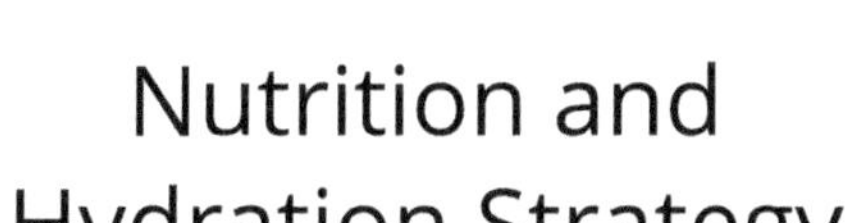

CHAPTER 8

Nutrition and Hydration Strategy

Fuel That Keeps You Moving Forward

Food is not just fuel in bikepacking.
Food is energy, recovery, morale, and decision-making power.

Under-fuel and everything becomes harder:

- Climbing feels impossible
- Navigation errors increase
- Mood drops
- Risk tolerance gets worse

Well-fed riders make better decisions. And good decisions keep trips safe and enjoyable.

The Reality of Bikepacking Calorie Burn

Most riders burn:
3,500 – 6,000 calories per day

This depends on:

-  Terrain
- Load weight
- Weather
- Fitness
- Ride duration

If you try to eat like you do at home, you will run out of energy fast.

The Bikepacking Nutrition Pyramid

Level 1 - Constant Snack Fuel

Eat small amounts every 45–60 minutes.

Examples:

- Trail mix
- Energy bars
- Bananas
- Wraps
- Peanut butter sachets

Level 2 - Real Meal Fuel

1–2 solid meals per day if possible.

Examples:

- Dehydrated meals
- Instant rice + tuna
- Pasta sides
- Supermarket ready meals (short trips)

Level 3 - Emergency Fuel

Always carry one "bonk recovery" food.

Examples:

- Chocolate
- Energy gel
- Sugary drink powder

> ⚡ **PRO TIP**
>
> If you feel suddenly emotional, weak, or unmotivated - eat immediately.
>
> Low energy often feels like low morale.

Hydration Strategy

Dehydration reduces performance faster than hunger.

Mild dehydration effects:

-  Headaches
- Poor concentration
- Slower reaction time

Water Planning Basics

Know where:

- Next confirmed water source
- Backup water options
- Daily water carry capacity

> ### 🌍 Real-World Example
>
> On a hot gravel route, a rider assumed a water tap at a campsite would work. It didn't. They had to ration water for 25 km to the next town. They finished safely - but it was preventable.
>
> Water assumptions are dangerous. Water confirmation is smart.

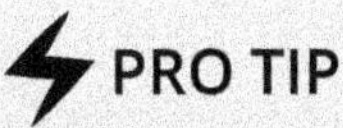

PRO TIP

Drink before you are thirsty

Thirst means dehydration has already started.

Pack food wisely

Do not pack food into every bag that you have

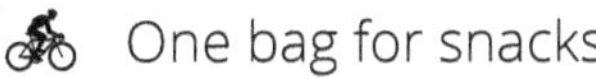

- 🚴 One bag for snacks
- 🚴 One bag for all other food, and if you can - toiletries and other animal attractants

If every bag has a lingering food aroma, this will encourage critters to nibble their way in to investigate while you sleep.

Easy access snacks

You should be able to access your snacks safely one handed while riding. A stem mounted food bag is ideal for this.

 ## Tales from the trails...

Being British, there are certain non-negotiables in life. One of them is tea. Proper tea. At multiple intervals throughout the day. Without it, everything starts to fall apart.

On one particular trip, my riding mate refused to carry milk powder. Apparently, a previous incident involving a bag of it exploding in a pannier had clearly left emotional scars.

So when we discovered condensed milk in a tube, it felt like innovation at its finest. Milk. In a tube. Pre-sweetened. Civilisation neatly packaged.

Yes, it did say "Keep refrigerated once opened."

But the expiry date was several years away. I took this to mean it was made purely of preservatives and probably had never have been anywhere near a cow. We reasoned that we'd use it quickly. It would be fine. Besides, how warm could it really get in a black saddle bag, sitting in direct sun, strapped to a bike all day?

What followed was a short but intense period during which I developed the ability to locate bushes at record speed. My digestive system became impressively punctual.

The tea was excellent. The consequences were not.

The moral of the story?

If a product suggests refrigeration, it is not offering a casual opinion. And black saddle bags in full sun are not, despite appearances, portable fridges.

Camp Craft and Sleep Systems

Recovery Is Performance

Many riders focus on riding performance - and ignore recovery performance.

Bad sleep = bad riding tomorrow.

Great sleep = stronger riding, better decisions, higher morale.

Campsite Selection Basics

Look for:

- Wind protection, but not under trees
- Flat ground that can take a tent peg
- Drainage (avoid water pooling)
- Distance from animal trails
- Safe distance from water flooding zones

Camp Setup Efficiency

Good camp systems aim for:

-  15 minute setup
-  10 minute morning pack down

Efficiency saves energy.

 *Real-World Example*

On a cold trip, two riders finished at the same time. One had a fast, rehearsed camp setup and was in their sleeping bag within 15 minutes. The other took 45 minutes setting up unfamiliar gear and got dangerously cold.

Practice saves energy - and sometimes increases safety.

Sleep Temperature Reality

Most people find sleep outdoors colder than expected.

If your bag rating is:
0°C comfort → expect comfort around 5°C for most riders.

 PRO TIP

If you are slightly too warm in your sleeping bag, you packed correctly.

If you are cold, recovery quality drops fast.

The Morale Factor

Tiny comforts matter:

-  Good pillow
- Dry socks
- Warm drink

Morale is performance fuel.

Food thieves

Whether you're deep in bear country or just at a local campsite, it's a good habit to keep yourself separate from anything that might smell edible - including toiletries.

A good rule is to maintain about 100 metres between where you sleep, where you cook, and where you store your food overnight.

And if you're in bear country, it's wise to store the clothes you cooked in with your food overnight. Hang them at least 4 metres up a tree and at least 2 metres out from the trunk or store them in a bear box if one is available.

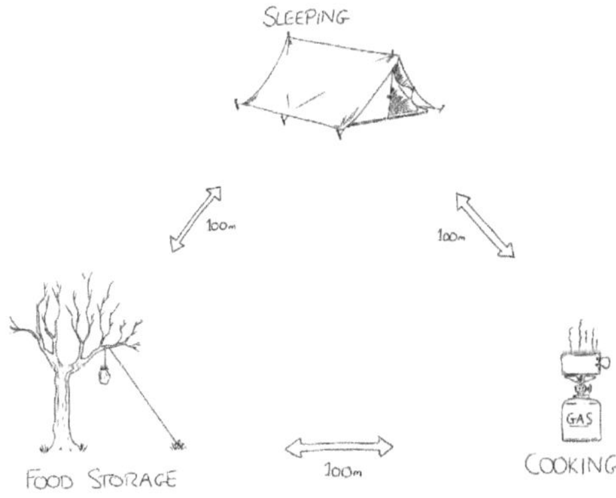

 *Tales from the trails...*

I met William - or Billy the Frog as he quickly became known - on a trip that involved long trails, questionable weather, and plenty of time to observe other people's packing decisions.

Billy looked like he'd been genetically engineered for cycling. Lean, long-legged, built like he should have been floating up climbs in the ranges. And yet... us older folk would power past him.

The reason became clear when we examined his bike.

Thirty kilograms of gear. 30.

Among the essentials was a laptop and charger. He explained that he might attend a job interview during the trip. He did indeed make it to the interview - dusty, mildly sunburnt, and with hair that had spent several weeks negotiating with a helmet. He didn't get the job.

His sleep system was equally optimistic. A 3m x 3m heavy-duty plastic tarp paired with a domestic inflatable mattress. Luxurious in theory. In practice, it offered no fly net and was more like a wind tunnel than a shelter.

Each morning Billy emerged looking like he'd lost a small but determined boxing match with nature.

You don't need the most expensive gear, but it does need to be fit for purpose.

CHAPTER 10

Daily Ride Strategy and Energy Management

Ride Smart, Not Just Strong

Bikepacking rewards consistency more than intensity.

Fast riders who burn out early often struggle more than steady riders.

The 60% Effort Rule

Ride most of the day with comfortable unquickened breathing, otherwise known as "Conversation pace".

You should feel like you *could* go harder - but choose not to.

Why This Works

Lower intensity:

 Preserves glycogen

Reduces muscle breakdown

Improves next-day recovery

Lowers injury risk

> ⚡ **PRO TIP**
>
> If you finish a day completely destroyed, the pacing was wrong - not the distance.

Break Strategy

Ideal pattern:
Ride 60–90 minutes
Break 5–10 minutes

Longer breaks reduce total distance and increase fatigue stiffness.

 *Real-World Example*

On a long gravel route, one rider sprinted climbs and rested long at stops. Another rode steady all day. The steady rider finished fresher and faster overall.

Consistency wins multi-day trips.

Weather Energy Management

Heat → reduce pace early

Cold → fuel more often

Wind → accept slower speed

Fighting the environment wastes energy.

Working with the environment saves energy.

> ⚡ **PRO TIP**
>
> Start slower than you think you should. You will pass people later.

The 4 mantra to bikepacking resilience

Mantra 1. Never ride past food, or water if in a desert!

 The resupply points you think you have may not be open, or even still in business!

- Even if they are, sometimes the amount of time it takes you to get to them is way longer than you think.

- You are always much hungrier than you thought possible as you are probably burning twice your normally calorie count for days on end.

Mantra 2. Ride today so you can ride tomorrow

This mantra was stolen from a surfer. Staying out in the surf for 'just one more wave' will inevitably result in getting tired, making a mistake and getting slammed into a sand bar.

- Check the depth of the stream you are about to cross
- Don't hammer the downhills
- The ambulance can't get to you for hours
- It's a long walk back
- Etc etc etc

There a million things to remember to either do, or not do to keep you in condition to be able to keep riding, instead of trying to remember them all, just repeat this mantra when making a decision.

Mantra 3. Stand up downhill

While cycling, your hands, feet, and backside are glued to the bike. The terrain you will be riding on is unlikely to be either flat or smooth. You will become fatigued. Make the most of the downhills to change your position.

- Stand up and stretch the back and neck
- Lighten the grip on the handlebars
- Let the backside have a break

Go as hard as you like up the hills but make the most of the downs and savour them while you can.

Mantra 4. Don't pedal if you don't have to

It sounds simple, but it is not an easy habit to adopt. To get to the point in life where you are going to undertake a bikepacking adventure, you have probably already programmed your brain to "just keep peddling". It's second nature, you pedal without thinking about it.

 Pedal for 10 revolutions, then coast

 Don't bother pedalling at all on slight declines

Bank all of those missed revolutions to have 'fresher' legs for tomorrow or push on a bit further down the track.

 *Tales from the trails...*

On Day One of the Great Divide Mountain Bike Route (northbound), we made what felt like a financially responsible decision.

Instead of spending $500 to travel down to Antelope Wells - the traditional starting point - we began in El Paso. Practical. Efficient. Sensible.

From there, we had options. Two manageable 80km days... or one bold, character-building 140km push to Deming. The profile suggested a very polite 200 metres of climbing. We were fresh. Optimistic. Fully hydrated and full of motivational phrases.

Naturally, we chose the big day.

What followed was less "steady introduction to an epic route" and more "immediate negotiation with reality."

- *Seventeen hours in the saddle.*
- *Afternoon headwinds clocking 60km/h directly in our faces.*
- *Multiple cactus punctures.*
- *162km ride distance.*

And, somehow, over 2000 metres of climbing - which was quite a surprise given the advertised 200, it turns out Komoot was not that trustworthy across unmapped desert tracks.

Day Two became an unplanned rest day, spent quietly reconsidering our relationship with ambition.

The route hadn't punished us. It had simply introduced itself properly. The lesson?

There is no prize for winning Day One. Start steady. Let the adventure unfold gradually. Your legs - and your morale - will thank you.

CHAPTER 11

Safety and Emergency Planning

Confidence Comes from Preparation

The goal of safety planning is not to eliminate all risk.

Adventure always contains uncertainty.

The goal is to remove **avoidable risk** and prepare for **manageable problems**.

Safe riders are not the ones who avoid challenges.

Safe riders are the ones who expect problems - and prepare solutions.

The Three Layers of Bikepacking Safety

Layer 1 - Prevention

Good planning prevents most emergencies.

Includes:

- Route research, resupply points, terrain
- Weather checking vs. sleep & clothing systems
- Fitness matching route difficulty
- Gear testing
- Water planning
- Maintenance skills

Layer 2 - Problem Management

When things go wrong, can you stabilise the situation?

Includes:

- First aid skills
- Mechanical repair skills
- Navigation backup
- Emergency shelter knowledge

Layer 3 - Emergency Communication

If everything goes wrong, can you call for help?

Includes:

-  Satellite messenger (remote trips)
- Trip plans left with trusted contacts
- Emergency numbers saved offline

> **⚡ PRO TIP**
>
> Most bikepacking emergencies start as small problems that get ignored.

Fix issues early - hot spots, strange bike noises, dehydration signs.

> **🌍 Real-World Example**
>
> *On a remote fire road, a rider ignored a small tyre wobble. Hours later, the tyre failed completely while far from help. A quick inspection earlier on would have prevented hours of walking.*
>
> *Small checks prevent big problems.*

Personal Risk Awareness

Ask daily:

- Am I tired enough to make bad decisions?
- Am I hydrated and fed?
- Is the weather changing faster than expected?

Self-awareness is a safety tool.

Emergency Plan

Calm Decisions Create Safe Outcomes

Every bikepacking trip deserves an emergency plan - not because you expect something to go wrong, but because preparation builds calm confidence.

When you know what to do, panic disappears.

This plan should be designed to be simple, realistic, and easy to remember.

Before You Leave

1. Share Your Route

Provide a trusted contact with:

- Planned route map (digital or printed)
- Start date and time
- Expected finish date and time

- Planned check-in schedule
- Emergency escalation instructions

Make sure they know when to act if you don't check in.

2. Set a Check-In Rule

Example:

"If you haven't heard from me by 9pm on Sunday, call me. If no response within 12 hours, contact local authorities."

Clarity prevents confusion.

3. Carry Essential Emergency Tools

Minimum recommended:

- Basic first aid kit
- Emergency contact numbers (offline)
- Backup navigation (paper or offline maps)
- Fully charged phone
- Satellite messenger for remote areas

If Something Goes Wrong

Step 1: Stop - Do not continue riding under stress or injury.

Step 2: Assess the situation, ask the questions:

- "Am I injured?"
- "Is the bike rideable?"
- "Do I have water and shelter?"

Slow thinking prevents escalation.

Step 3: Stabilise

If there is an injury:

- Control bleeding
- Prevent further movement
- Add insulation to avoid shock

If mechanical:

- Move off trail
- Diagnose calmly
- Use repair kit methodically

Step 4: Decide

You have three options:

- Self-repair and continue
- Adjust route to nearest exit

🚲 Activate emergency contact device

Choosing early is strength, not weakness.

Weather Emergency Protocol

If severe weather approaches:

🚲 Stop early

🚲 Make camp below ridgelines

🚲 Avoid exposed high points

🚲 Add insulation immediately

Waiting out weather is often smarter than pushing through it.

The Golden Rule

Minor problems become emergencies when ignored.

Fix small issues early:

🚲 Hot spots on feet

🚲 Strange mechanical noises

🚲 Low water levels

🚲 Fatigue symptoms

Prevention is the most powerful safety strategy.

The Confidence Reminder

Preparation does not make adventure smaller.

It makes you stronger within it.

When you carry a plan, you carry calm.

And calm riders make good decisions.

CHAPTER 12

Weather, Terrain and Environmental Risk

Work With Nature, Not Against It

Nature never negotiates.
Smart riders learn to cooperate with it.

The Three Most Common Environmental Risks

1. Heat

Danger signs:

 Headache
 Nausea
 Irritability
 Sudden fatigue

2. Cold and Hypothermia

Danger signs:

- Shivering
- Slurred speech
- Poor coordination
- Confusion

3. Storm Systems

Danger signs:

- Sudden temperature drop
- Fast wind direction changes
- Dark vertical cloud build-up

 **PRO TIP**

If weather makes you question continuing - stop early, not late.

 *Real-World Example*

A rider once pushed into an incoming storm to "make distance". They had to make an emergency shelter, lost hours drying out gear. Stopping early and making camp in calmer conditions would have saved energy and stress.

Distance is optional. Safety is not.

Terrain Risk Awareness

Watch for:

 Loose descents

 Washed-out roads

 River crossing depth changes

 Wildlife zones

 *Tales from the trails...*

There is absolutely no rule in bikepacking that says you must make life harder than necessary.

One of my regular riding mates (let's call him 'Adam' to confirm his identity) appears to believe there is.

He treats certain trail features - particularly stream crossings - as if they are personal challenges issued directly by nature. As the water flows across the trail, he seems to hear a call: "I dare you."

My approach is somewhat less dramatic - but time consuming.

When I reach a stream crossing, I stop. I look at it. I study it as though I'm considering a property purchase.

How deep is it?

How fast is it moving?

Are those stable stones, or are they the sort that move under the front wheel at precisely the wrong moment?

And perhaps most importantly - how cold is it?

If it's more than about six inches deep - and especially if it's glacier-fed and enthusiastic - I take off my riding shoes and socks, hang them around my neck, and I then walk through calmly.

Yes, my feet get wet.

Yes, I am briefly cold. But a quick dry with my buff and then I have dry warm feet again and I don't spend the rest of the day marinating them in icy regret.

Adam?

No hesitation. No reconnaissance. He charges straight in, pedals furiously, emerges victorious… and then squelches for the next five hours.

Cold. Wet. Determined.

I've never fully understood the appeal.

Sometimes, adventure is about resilience.

And sometimes, it's simply about taking your shoes off.

CHAPTER 13

Mechanical Survival Skills

Your Bike Is Your Lifeline

Mechanical confidence reduces stress massively.

You don't need to be a professional mechanic.

You do need to solve:

- Punctures
- Chain issues
- Brake adjustments
- Loose bolts
- Gear indexing problems

The Non-Negotiable Field Repair Skills

Learn before remote trips:

-  Tube or tubeless puncture repairs
- Chain quick link removal / install
- Brake pad checks and replacement
- Brake adjustment
- Tyre boot repair
- Gear indexing problems

 **PRO TIP**

If you can fix it in your garage, you can fix it on the trail - if you bring the right tools.

 *Real-World Example*

One rider carried a chain tool for years but never practised using it. When a chain snapped on a trip, stress made the repair harder. Practising once would have made it routine.

Skill + calm = fast effective fix.

Preventative Maintenance Is the Secret Weapon

Before an adventure, invest in:

- New or near-new tyres
- Fresh brake pads
- Chain health check
- Bolt torque check
- Crank / bearings

Most mechanical failures are predictable.

Staying Calm When Things Go Sideways

Most trail-side problems are manageable with patience and a little practical knowledge.

The key is not speed - it's calm assessment.

Here are a few common situations and how to think your way through them.

Partial Derailleur Failure

Sometimes a derailleur becomes bent after a minor knock, or a wireless unit may lose communication and stop shifting properly. In many cases, the derailleur isn't completely broken - it's simply stuck in one gear.

If that gear is manageable, you may choose to continue riding gently to the next town. If it isn't practical, there are ways to adjust it temporarily.

With a cable-actuated system, you can carefully loosen the cable bolt and either release or increase tension until the derailleur settles into a more usable gear. Small adjustments make a difference, so move gradually and reassess as you go.

With a wireless derailleur that has stopped responding, riders have improvised by gently repositioning the derailleur body to align with a suitable cog. In some cases, something like a spare spoke or cable tie has been used to hold it in place temporarily. This is not elegant - but it can get you home.

The goal isn't perfection. It's functionality.

Complete Derailleur Failure

A direct rock strike or severe damage can render a derailleur unusable. If that happens, the most reliable solution is often to convert your bike temporarily into a single-speed setup.

This involves removing the damaged derailleur and shortening the chain so it runs directly between the front chainring and a chosen rear cog.

Choosing the right rear cog is important - something roughly mid-range will usually give you a manageable compromise between climbing and flat terrain. The chain must be shortened appropriately to maintain tension.

It won't be fast. It may not be graceful. But it can be enough to finish your route or reach assistance.

Gear Indexing in the Field

Before adjusting anything, it's worth pausing to clean your drivetrain. Grit, dust, and debris are common causes of poor shifting. A quick wipe of the chain, cassette, and jockey wheels can sometimes restore smooth performance without further adjustment.

For wireless drivetrains, indexing is usually automatic. Minor trim adjustments can often be made through the companion app (such as SRAM or Shimano systems), if needed.

For cable-driven systems, begin by shifting to the smallest rear cog. If you're running a two-by setup at the front, shift to the larger chainring. If you have a triple chainring, the middle ring is the correct position.

From there, gently wind in the barrel adjuster to reduce cable tension. Loosen the cable anchor bolt at the derailleur, remove any slack from the cable, and retighten it carefully.

You can then begin testing the indexing. Shift one gear at a time while turning the pedals, listening for smooth, clean movement. If the chain hesitates or sounds strained, make small barrel adjuster adjustments and test again.

There is often a small "window" where shifting feels good. You're looking for that balanced point.

Take your time. Rushed adjustments rarely improve things.

Removing a Chain Without a Chain Breaker

If your chain uses a quick link, you have options even without a dedicated chain tool.

One simple method involves positioning the quick link at the top of the chainring so it's easily accessible. With the chain slightly tensioned, you can gently tap the quick link with a multi-tool until it releases.

To reinstall, reconnect the quick link and rotate it to the top section of the chain. Applying firm pedal pressure will usually snap it securely into place.

It may take patience, but it's entirely achievable on the trail.

It isn't ugly if it works

Field repairs are rarely neat. They are often improvised, slightly random, and occasionally frustrating.

But every mechanical problem you solve adds confidence that stays with you long after the trip ends.

You don't need to be a professional mechanic. You only need enough knowledge to stay calm, think clearly, and take the next practical step.

And more often than not, that's enough to keep the adventure moving forward.

 ***Tales from the trails...***

Before a long, multi-week overseas ride, my riding partner and I decided to do the sensible thing and switch to running our tyres tubeless right from the start of our training block.

Responsible. Methodical. Mature.

We'd both had enough punctures in the past to appreciate the benefits, and over the weeks we became reasonably competent at inserting "bacon strips" into offending holes. At first, we fumbled like trainee surgeons but eventually, we developed a smooth little routine: locate hole, plug hole, reinflate, carry on looking mildly heroic.

By departure time, we felt confident.

We landed overseas, rebuilt our bikes, and quite wisely decided to go for a short shake-down ride before heading into the mountains.

Which is when my mate rolled over a nail.

Not a polite little thorn. A substantial, centre-line, fully committed nail.

"No problem," we thought. Out came the bacon strip kit. Repair inserted. Pump applied.

The tyre refused to hold air.

We tried again. And again. After half an hour of gentle optimism fading into sticky sealant-covered resignation, we admitted defeat and converted the wheel back to an inner tube. Out came the tubeless valve. Out came the fresh goo.

We then made an urgent pilgrimage to a local bike shop, where the mystery was solved: the nail had passed neatly through the tyre, and directly through the rim tape at a spoke hole.

A one-in-a-million shot.

Rim tape replaced, tyre converted back to tubeless, and we were back in business - slightly humbler, slightly messier.

The lesson?

Sometimes you need a backup to your backup.

Especially when that small strip of rubber is the only thing standing between you and walking.

Peanut Butter Mud

This amazingly self-adhesive mud is more common than you might think. You are likely to encounter it at least once on a ride lasting more than a week if you're travelling in a damp climate.

Within 20 metres, your tyres can go from slightly gritty to twice their normal size. Your frame will scrape the mud off and drop it onto your chainring and cassette. You will likely drop the chain and/or jam the jockey wheels in your rear derailleur. It's terrible stuff.

The only way to remove it is with copious amounts of water - a precious resource you need to survive.

Avoiding the situation (when possible) is the best approach. If you notice the mud beginning to build up, stop quickly, get off the bike, step to the side of the track, and walk the section on the scrub or grass at the trail edge.

Walk as long as you need to, trying to ride too early will cause nothing but regret.

If you pass a stream, use the free-flowing water to rinse off the mud and then reoil or rewax your drivetrain.

CHAPTER 14

When the Trail Gets Technical

Riding Skills That Expand Your World

At some point, every bikepacker reaches a section of trail that looks intimidating.

- Loose rocks
- Steep descents
- Sand
- River crossings

This is where growth happens.

Technical riding is not about aggression. It is about control.

And control comes from skill, not bravery.

The Confidence Equation

Skill + Vision + Relaxation = Control

If one of those breaks down, tension increases.
When tension increases, mistakes follow.

Descending Loose Terrain

Key principles:

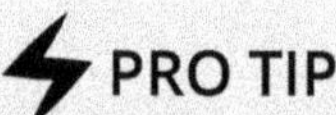 Lower your centre of gravity

- Look ahead, not at your front wheel

- Light hands, heavy feet

- Brake before corners, not in them

Your bike wants to stay upright. Trust it.

> ⚡ **PRO TIP**
>
> If you feel tense descending, you are likely gripping too hard.
>
> Shake out your hands. Reset your breathing.

Climbing Technical Sections

- Stay seated when possible
- Keep weight centred
- Maintain steady cadence
- Accept slower progress

Momentum is more important than speed.

Sand and Soft Surfaces

Sand feels unstable because it shifts beneath tyres.

Technique:

- Lower tyre pressure slightly
- Stay relaxed
- Keep pedalling smoothly
- Avoid sharp steering corrections

The more you fight sand, the more it wins.

 *Real-World Example*

On a long sandy river trail, one rider repeatedly tried to power through aggressively and burned out fast. Another rider reduced tyre pressure slightly, relaxed, and rode smoother lines. Same terrain. Completely different energy outcomes.

Efficiency beats force.

River Crossings

Always:

- Check depth before riding
- Walk if unsure
- Keep drivetrain elevated if possible
- Dry chain afterwards

Adventure is not worth a damaged drivetrain.

Expanding Your Comfort Zone

Every technical section you ride safely increases your range.

The goal is not to conquer terrain.
The goal is to expand what feels normal.
That's how your world grows.

 *Tales from the trails...*

I'll happily admit this: I am not the most technically gifted rider.

My regular riding crew, on the other hand, seem perfectly at home in rock gardens, tight twisty singletrack, loose gravel, washboards - essentially anything that isn't smooth, champagne gravel. They float. They glide. They descend with the relaxed confidence of people who trust both their bikes and their reflexes.

For a long time, we all ran almost identical setups. Same tyre widths. Same rigid seatposts. Same style and placement of packs. On paper, we were perfectly matched.

Climbing wasn't the problem. I could grind uphill alongside them without much drama. Although I did manage to fall off going up a 12% hill at 3kmh once, as I said, not gifted.

Descending was a different story.

While they flowed down technical sections, I was negotiating. Braking. Occasionally providing unintentional entertainment. They would kindly wait at the bottom, trying not to look too comfortable while I rolled in, slightly rattled and very aware of the time gap.

Eventually, it dawned on me: perhaps it wasn't entirely a talent issue.

I switched to wider tyres, lowered the pressures, and added a dropper post. Suddenly, the bike felt calmer. So did I. The same trails became less like survival exercises and more like actual riding.

The lesson wasn't about keeping up.

It was about building a system that works for you and the terrain you ride - not simply copying what everyone else happens to run.

Your setup should build confidence, not erode it.

CHAPTER 15

Beyond the Weekend

Planning Real Expeditions

A weekend trip builds confidence.
A multi-week trip builds identity.

Longer expeditions require a shift in thinking.

You are no longer planning a ride.
You are planning a mobile lifestyle.

The Five Expedition Planning Layers

1. Route architecture

2. Resupply rhythm

3. Maintenance intervals

4. Budget planning

5. Recovery days

Route Architecture

Break long routes into:

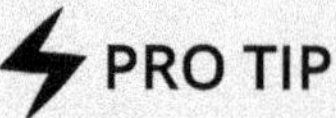

- Logical sections
- Natural resupply towns
- Terrain difficulty phases

Don't look at 1,000 km as one ride.
Look at it as 10 manageable segments.

⚡ **PRO TIP**

Plan rest days before you need them.

Rest days are not weakness.

They are strategy.

Resupply Rhythm

Long trips require mental structure.

Example rhythm:

- Ride 3–4 days
- Resupply
- Laundry
- Recharge devices
- Repeat

Structure reduces decision fatigue.

>  ***Real-World Example***
>
> *On a 2-week gravel route, one rider rode until exhaustion before resting. Another scheduled recovery days every fourth day. The second rider finished stronger and happier.*
>
> *Planning rest is not quitting.*
> *It's leadership over your own energy.*

Budget Awareness

Longer trips require:

- 🚲 Food budgeting
- 🚲 Accommodation buffer
- 🚲 Emergency transport fund

Financial stress ruins adventure quickly.

Plan margins.

Train for the Ride You Want to Finish

How to prepare Your Body and Mind for a Two-Week Bikepacking Adventure?

A two-week bikepacking journey isn't just a long ride. It's a series of long rides, stacked day after day, while carrying gear, adapting to terrain, and recovering each evening so you can do it again tomorrow.

The good news is that you still don't need to be an elite cyclist to succeed. What you do need is more durability - the kind that allows you to ride steadily, wake up the next morning, and feel capable of continuing.

That kind of resilience can be built deliberately and confidently.

This training plan is designed to help you arrive at your trip feeling prepared - not pressured.

Understanding the Goal of Training

It's easy to assume you should train for speed or power. In reality, most successful bikepackers rely far more on consistency than intensity or speed.

Your focus over the training weeks should be on:

- 🚲 Building a comfortable aerobic base
- 🚲 Adapting your body to time in the saddle
- 🚲 Strengthening key muscle groups
- 🚲 Learning to fuel and hydrate properly
- 🚲 Developing confidence riding on tired legs

If you can finish a long ride feeling like you could have gone a little further, you're training correctly.

A 12-week training plan is sufficient for a two-week ride.

This plan is divided into three phases. Each phase builds gently on the one before it, allowing progress without overload.

Phase 1: Building the Foundation (Weeks 1–4)

During the first month, your goal is to establish routine and aerobic fitness.

Each week might include:

- Two shorter rides of 60–90 minutes at an easy, conversational pace
- One longer ride of 2–3 hours
- One strength session focused on full-body stability
- An optional recovery spin, walk, or mobility session

At this stage, resist the urge to push hard. You should be able to talk comfortably while riding. This builds the endurance engine that will carry you through long days later.

No need for sprint training

If you find yourself breathing hard enough that conversation becomes difficult, you're likely riding harder than necessary. Endurance develops best when effort is controlled.

Phase 2: Adding Strength and Load (Weeks 5–8)

Once your base feels stable, you can begin adding more challenge.

This is when hills become more intentional, and your longer ride might extend to 3–4 hours. It's also the ideal time to start riding with some of your bikepacking load.

Begin gradually. Extra weight changes how the bike handles and how your body feels. Your shoulders, hands, and hips need time to adapt.

A typical week in this phase could include:

- 🚴 One hill-focused session
- 🚴 One steady mid-length endurance ride
- 🚴 One longer weekend ride with gear
- 🚴 One strength session
- 🚴 One easy recovery ride

Real-World Perspective

Many riders are surprised by how different a loaded bike feels. It isn't just heavier - it responds differently. The more familiar that feeling becomes before your expedition, the calmer you'll feel when the terrain becomes challenging.

Phase 3: Simulating the Real Thing (Weeks 9–12)

In the final month, training becomes more specific.

This is when back-to-back long rides become valuable. Riding four to six hours on a Saturday and then riding again the next day, even for a shorter duration, teaches your body to perform while carrying fatigue.

It's less about distance and more about how you recover overnight.

During these weeks, you'll learn:

- 🚲 How your nutrition affects the next day
- 🚲 How pacing influences soreness
- 🚲 How sleep impacts energy
- 🚲 How your mindset responds to accumulated effort

This is where confidence is built.

Benchmarks Before You Leave

Before beginning your two-week adventure, it's helpful to feel comfortable riding:

- 🚲 Five to six hours with gear
- 🚲 Two longer days back-to-back

You don't need to finish those rides exhausted. In fact, feeling steady and composed is a better sign than feeling drained.

The Mental Side of Preparation

Training isn't just physical.

Consider occasionally riding in less-than-perfect conditions. A light rain ride, a windy day, or a longer climb than usual can all build confidence. Exposure reduces anxiety.

When something feels manageable in training, it feels far less intimidating on your trip.

It's time to fly the nest

You may never feel completely ready. That's normal.

But if you've built consistency, practised riding with load, learned to fuel yourself properly, and experienced riding on tired legs - you are more prepared than you think.

A two-week bikepacking trip isn't conquered through raw strength.

It's completed through steady effort, thoughtful pacing, and the quiet confidence that you've done the work.

And that confidence is built long before the first day of your adventure.

Note: A 4-week ride would not need double the training, add an extra two weeks into phase 2 and another two into phase 3 to give you a 16-week training plan.

CHAPTER 16

International and
Remote Bikepacking

There is something powerful about riding into places where your language isn't spoken and your comfort zone shrinks.

Remote bikepacking magnifies everything:

- Reward
- Risk
- Beauty
- Responsibility

Remote Risk Amplification

In remote regions:

- Help is farther away
- Weather changes matter more
- Mechanical failure consequences increase

Your preparation must scale with remoteness.

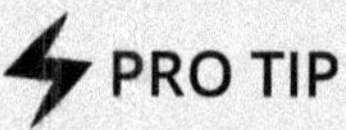

PRO TIP

If your risk increases, your conservatism should increase too.

Ride smoother.
Descend slower.
Inspect gear more often.

Tales from the trails

Altitude. I live at sea level. My lungs are accustomed to thick, generous, oxygen filled air.

So, when I signed up for a long remote ride where the minimum altitude was 2,200 metres and we topped out at 3,600 metres, I assumed it would simply feel… slightly higher. Great views I imagined.

It did not feel slightly higher.

It felt like someone had turned the oxygen setting down to "economy mode."

The first morning, I sat up in my tent and immediately needed a moment. Putting on socks required a small recovery break. Tying shoelaces became an event. I'm fairly sure I burned more calories brushing my teeth than I had during some interval sessions back home.

Climbing hills? I can only say (in between gasps) - Ouch.

The strange thing about altitude is that nothing dramatic necessarily happens - you just feel mildly substandard at everything. Heart rate up. Breathing heavy. Pride slightly dented.

After a couple of weeks, my body began to adapt. Efforts felt steadier. Mornings no longer resembled high-intensity workouts.

But if you live at sea level and plan to ride high, consider this your gentle warning: the mountains do not care how fit you are at home.

They operate on different air.

And at 3,600 metres, even your shoelaces can humble you.

Why Remote Riding Feels So Powerful

When services disappear, self-reliance grows.

When landscapes stretch empty, perspective expands.

Remote riding doesn't just test skills - it reveals character.

And you will discover you are more capable than you believed.

International Riding - Taking Your Adventure Overseas

By the time you begin planning an overseas bikepacking trip, you will hopefully have a few domestic adventures behind you. Those early trips quietly refine your systems - your packing, your pacing, your routines.

International riding isn't dramatically different. In fact, most of the core principles remain the same.

There are simply a few additional layers to think through carefully and calmly.

Before international trips:

- 🚴 Research customs
- 🚴 Understand land access rules
- 🚴 Respect environmental protection laws
- 🚴 Learn basic phrases

Logistics

If you're travelling by air, your bike will need to be packed in either a dedicated bike bag or a cardboard bike box.

Bike bags come in two main forms: hard shell and soft. Both offer excellent protection. Hard shell cases provide slightly more impact resistance, but they are heavier and bulkier to move around. Soft bags are lighter and easier to store, and they still protect your bike well when packed properly.

Cardboard boxes are often available free from local bike shops, and some airlines sell them at check-in. They are perfectly workable but require thoughtful packing. You'll need to ensure that sharp components - such as chainrings or axle ends - are padded so they don't press through the cardboard, particularly if the box becomes damp in transit.

Then there is the return journey to consider.

If you travel with a cardboard box, you can usually dispose of it on arrival and source another at your departure location. If you bring your own bike bag, you'll need to organise storage or courier logistics so it is waiting for you at the end of your ride.

None of these challenges are insurmountable. They simply need to be part of your planning rather than an afterthought.

It's also wise to check visa requirements, permitted length of stay, and whether proof of onward travel is required before entering a country or crossing borders mid-route.

Small administrative oversights can create big interruptions.

Which Side of the Road (or Trail)?

When riding internationally, it's surprisingly easy to forget that traffic conventions differ from country to country.

On remote dirt roads or mountain trails, this may not feel significant. But when descending or cornering, local riders and drivers will instinctively expect you to be on a particular side.

Make it a habit to corner on the correct side of the trail, especially on blind bends. Even in quiet regions, you are rarely as alone as you think.

It's a small adjustment that prevents unnecessary risk.

Food and the Adventurous Stomach

One of the great joys of international riding is discovering new food, meeting new people, and experiencing local culture from the saddle.

Your enthusiasm, however, may occasionally outpace your digestive system.

An unsettled stomach while riding can quickly lead to dehydration and fatigue. It's rarely dramatic - just uncomfortable and energy-draining.

When you arrive in a new country, consider easing in. Try new foods but allow your body time to adjust. Stay hydrated. Notice how you feel.

There is no medal for sampling everything on day one.

It's the same planet

International bikepacking often feels like a leap into something larger and more uncertain. In reality, it is simply an extension of the skills you've already built.

Plan carefully. Respect local systems. Give your body time to adapt.

The fundamentals remain the same: steady pacing, thoughtful preparation, and an openness to learning.

The world becomes remarkably accessible when approached one pedal stroke at a time.

CHAPTER 17

Detailed Gear + Bike Breakdown

At the start of this book, we mentioned that the best bike to begin with is the one you already own, and the best gear is what you can depend on.

Over time, the bike and equipment you start your bikepacking adventures with will begin to wear out or reveal their limitations. When the time comes to upgrade, replace, or even build a completely new setup, this section will help inform your decisions and guide you toward creating something more tailored to you.

This chapter dives deeply into each component of a bikepacking setup, including the bike itself. The equipment described here will be capable of taking you almost anywhere on epic adventures.

Safety First – Tracking

How do you want to share your location, confirm you are OK, or signal if you need help?

Satellite Trackers

These are the ultimate option and especially useful if you will be in the wilderness for extended periods. They all feature an SOS button for emergencies and typically require a subscription plan, which triggers a response from local emergency services.

These devices can transmit your location without cell coverage, and some allow basic two-way messaging with the appropriate plan. They are often mandatory for organised events if you want your result officially recognised.

Example products: Spot Gen 4, Garmin inReach.

Smartphone

The next level down is a smartphone. Newer models (e.g., iPhone 16 onwards) can send your location via satellite, and in some countries two-way satellite messaging is available with the correct service plan.

Any Cell Phone

The minimum requirement is a standard phone with a local or roaming plan. As long as you reach cell reception, you can call for help.

Store key numbers in advance - local police, hospitals, and embassies if overseas.

First Aid Kit

Painkillers (anti-inflammatories are most useful), breathable plasters, a small tube of antiseptic cream, a crepe bandage, and a compression bandage. Depending on allergies: antihistamines, EpiPens, asthma inhalers. In remote areas: a space blanket and a whistle.

Water Management

There are two key considerations:

How much water do you need to carry?

How safe is it to drink?

Hot climates: minimum 3 litres per day until resupply.

Cool climates: minimum 1 litre per day until resupply.

Soft, flexible bladders save space and weight.

Example brands: MSR, HydraPak, Sea to Summit.

Water purification: filter, tablets, or boil all water - even tap water. An upset stomach on a bike is miserable.

Example filters: Lifestraw, Hydrapak, Sawyer, Katadyn BeFree.

Example tablets: Sawyer, Katadyn, Aquatabs.

Punctures

On multi-week rides, punctures are likely.

The optimal setup is tubeless tyres with correct sealant levels, plugs, spare sealant, and a spare valve.

If running tubes, carry two spares plus a quality repair kit.

For rough terrain, include tyre boots, vulcanising glue, and sandpaper to prepare surfaces.

Tyre levers and a pump are essential. CO_2 cartridges are impractical as tyre pressures require frequent adjustment, so carry a dependable pump.

Broken Spokes

Carry either spare spokes (front/rear, drive/non-drive may differ) or temporary options like FibreFix Kevlar spokes. These are lighter, easier to store, and require no special tools.

Note: Replacing a rear drive-side spoke requires removing the cassette, which needs another special tool. Not necessary with FibreFix.

Damaged Chains

Carry two or three spare links and ensure your multitool has a chain breaker. For long remote trips, consider a spare chain.

Rear Hanger

This small component connects the derailleur to the frame and is designed to break to protect the derailleur. They bend or snap easily - carry a spare.

Batteries

Electronic shifting is becoming common. Carry spares (e.g., CR2032 batteries for SRAM shifters).

Brakes

Disc brakes are essential. Larger rotors are preferable. Heavy loads and long descents wear pads quickly. Carry spare pads and the tools to replace them.

Cables

For mechanical setups, carry spare shift and brake cables. Add a craft knife and cable ties.

Straps

Things tend to work themselves loose on a bikepacking trip. Having a selection of straps to deal with this is well worth it.

Carry a small assortment of cable ties, straps, and cord. More often than not, you'll use all of them at some point during the trip. This is something to experiment with on your practice overnight rides: which options are easiest to pack and provide the most utility for your setup?

Rubber straps:
Available in various lengths, slightly stretchy rubber straps (e.g. Voile-style straps) are ideal for keeping larger pieces of luggage stable.

Cable ties:
Carry a small, medium, and large size selection. They take up very little space, are quick to deploy, and offer significant strength for securing items together.

Velcro rolls/straps:
Super light and easy to pack. A 50 cm roll can be cut up with a craft knife as required. I nearly always end up using the entire roll.

Canvas straps:
Thin (about 1 cm wide) but long (around 1 m), cotton or canvas-style straps with a simple aluminium clasp are also very light and easy to store. They offer excellent flexibility for preventing items from shifting.

Rubber bungee loops:
Stretchy, soft rubber loops (approximately 30 cm in diameter) are very handy for securing occasional items - for example, keeping a rain jacket attached to your front roll bag. They allow fast, easy access and cope very well with constant vibrations.

Maintenance Equipment

Make cleaning your bike a daily habit. A maintained bike is rideable; a neglected one gets pushed.

Keep the drivetrain clean with a brush. Wax (e.g. Squirt) attracts less dirt than oil-based lubricants.

Check brake rotors, pads, and axle tightness daily.

Clothing

Let's work from the ground up - starting with your feet.

Shoes

The two most practical options are mountain bike shoes with SPD-style cleats, or flat hiking shoes.

SPD shoes require compatible SPD pedals. The advantage is that you stay connected to the bike over rough terrain, especially at speed. The downside is limited foot movement, which can increase numbness over long hours. They are also less comfortable during inevitable "hike-a-bike" sections.

Flat, low-cut hiking shoes paired with wide platform pedals are often more comfortable for walking and evening / camp use. However, your feet can slip off in technical sections, which can be unsettling - and occasionally painful.

Waterproof options (e.g., Gore-Tex) are usually worthwhile. Some riders prefer robust sandals (e.g., Teva), with or without socks, for breathability.

Consider climate and personal preference carefully. For socks, merino wool is hard to beat.

Shorts / Underwear

Two main approaches: padded Lycra shorts or traditional underwear with walking shorts.

Padded shorts can be more comfortable, particularly if saddle time in training has been limited. However, they trap bacteria, are harder to wash and dry, and usually require carrying two pairs.

An alternative is merino underwear with durable shorts. This is easier to keep clean but can be tougher on the backside.

A compromise: take one of each and alternate.

Shirt / Torso

Long exposure to the elements demands quality layers.

A collared shirt offers better sun protection than a standard T-shirt. Fabric choice depends on environment. A merino base layer, merino T-shirt, and lightweight collared overshirt cover most needs.

Sun sleeves help when UV levels exceed what sunscreen can manage. In colder conditions, double up base layers and swap sun sleeves for arm warmers.

Jacket

A high-quality waterproof jacket quickly becomes indispensable. It blocks wind and handles most rain.

Consider compatibility with headwear. If wearing a helmet, ensure the hood fits over it to prevent water running down your back. Wearing a helmet over a hood can restrict hearing and feel uncomfortable - though some riders prefer it.

Head

A buff is extremely versatile - managing sweat, covering your neck, and adding light padding under a helmet.

Helmet

A mountain bike helmet provides extra coverage and usually includes a visor. An additional peak can help with glare.

While bikepacking speeds are generally lower, resupply sections involve traffic. Wearing a helmet consistently is simpler than trying to find somewhere to strap it to your bike.

That said - riding briefly without a helmet in a safe environment can be a refreshing reminder of why you ride.

Sunglasses

Essential. Polarised lenses divide opinion - personal preference rules here.

If you wear prescription glasses, consider transition bifocals to reduce the need for multiple pairs.

Suncream

Critical, especially early in a trip. Severe sunburn not only increases skin cancer risks but disrupts sleep and comfort.

A 50ml tube is usually sufficient for the first week. As your skin adapts, usage may decrease.

Hands

Many bikepackers skip gloves. Gloves primary function is warmth rather than comfort.

Thick gloves reduce dexterity. Waterproof gloves often fail in sustained rain.

A practical solution: thin wool or fleece gloves, paired with oversized rubber gloves (e.g. washing up gloves) in wet conditions. Tuck rubber cuffs under your jacket sleeves to prevent water ingress.

Camp Clothing

If racing, minimal clothing is required.

Otherwise, balance comfort with weight and space. Lightweight trousers that convert into shorts are highly practical. Evening biting insects make leg coverage useful.

Fresh underwear improves morale. A lightweight fleece is a valuable luxury. In near-freezing temperatures, it doubles as sleepwear.

Camp shoes: lightweight flip-flops are usually sufficient. Some riders prefer sandals and also use for occasional riding.

Sleep Mats

Quality sleep rivals food and water in importance.

Two main options: foam eggshell mats and inflatable mats.

Foam mats are durable and puncture-proof but bulky and less comfortable. Most have an R-value around 2 (adequate to ~0°C).

Inflatable mats are more comfortable and often warmer (R-values up to 5), but prone to punctures.

Layering foam under inflatable can increase insulation and reduce puncture risk - though not always successfully.

Sleeping Bags

Buy the best you can afford. Higher price typically means better warmth-to-weight ratio and packability.

Sleeping bag liners add hygiene and comfort and are easier to wash than sleeping bags.

Down bags are warmer and lighter but difficult to dry if wet. Synthetic bags are heavier but tolerate moisture better.

Pillow

A small inflatable pillow improves sleep dramatically. Alternatively, use a small pillowcase stuffed with clothing.

Shelter (Tent, Bivvy, Tarp, Hammock)

I like to plan routes with resupply every four or five days - ideally including a night in a real bed. A hot shower and a proper mattress become genuine luxuries after several days in the wilderness.

For the remaining nights, your shelter must keep you warm, dry, and properly rested.

Tent

The most common option. Many manufacturers now offer bikepacking-specific versions of lightweight or ultralight tents, featuring shorter poles and compact storage systems that strap neatly to the bike.

Sharing a tent allows riders to split poles, flysheet, and inner to balance weight. However, some ultralight single-person tents are lighter than shared setups and offer valuable personal space.

Bivvy

The "human burrito" option can be even lighter and more compact than a tent. However, entry and exit can be awkward, and they may feel claustrophobic - particularly in bad weather when fabric gets pressed against your face in strong winds.

Some racers choose ultralight bivvies for minimal protection from insects and weather while prioritising speed and simplicity.

Hammock

Hammocks work brilliantly for some riders, but for most people they are cold, uncomfortable, and finding suitable anchor points every night is unrealistic.

If you choose this option, test it thoroughly beforehand. Some hammocks include integrated insect screens. Rain protection always requires a separate tarp.

Tarp

A flat sheet with reinforced eyelets. Lightweight and space-efficient, it provides rain and limited wind protection.

The downside: no insect barrier. Expect bites in midge-heavy environments.

Food System

Before choosing food, decide whether you need to cook at all.

Carrying a stove, fuel, and cookware adds weight and bulk. If daily access to cooked food is likely, consider leaving the stove behind.

If not, here are the main options:

Gas (Butane, Propane, Blended)

All are clean, fast, and controllable.
Butane struggles in cold weather.
Propane performs better in cold but requires heavier canisters.
Butane/Propane blends provide balanced performance.

At altitude, output declines as canisters empty. Test with a partially used canister before longer trips.

Liquid Fuel (White Gas)

Reliable in cold and at altitude. Burns cleanly but requires priming and careful handling. Fuel spills can be hazardous.

Multi-Fuel (Diesel, Petrol, Kerosene)

Widely available and dependable. Downsides include soot production, odour, and heavier fuel weight. Leaks can contaminate gear.

Alcohol

Lightweight and quiet but slower to boil. Requires carrying additional fuel.

Sticks / Biomass Stoves

Use local twigs and leaf litter. Excellent in dry conditions and eliminate fuel carrying. However, ineffective in wet weather and often prohibited during fire bans.

Cookware

Titanium pots are ideal: light, durable, and easy to clean. Choose a size that fits your fuel system efficiently.

Most riders use a single 'spork' rather than full cutlery.

Plate

Often unnecessary. Eating directly from the cooking vessel reduces cleaning and saves space.

Cup

A simple plastic beaker is often most practical. Titanium cools quickly; enamel and steel add weight. Collapsible silicone versions may fail over time.

Food

A six-hour riding day may require 4,000–6,000 calories.

Expect hunger. Over multi-week rides, weight loss is common despite frequent eating.

Balance carbohydrates (energy), protein (repair), and fibre (digestion). Supplements depend on individual needs.

Plan for essentials; unexpected treats boost morale.

Breakfast

Porridge or muesli provides strong carbohydrate foundations. Powdered milk is practical; condensed milk spoils quickly.

Tea or coffee supports hydration and routine.

Lunch

Often lighter - snacks combined with fruit if it survives transport.

Dinner

If not heading to town, aim to stop two to three hours before sunset.

Pitch shelter first. Storms arrive unexpectedly.

Meals typically centre on dried rice, pasta, or potato with added protein (tuna, ham, jerky). Simple food becomes deeply satisfying after long days.

Dried fruit or remaining fresh fruit makes a practical dessert.

Snacks

Hard candy prevents dry mouth and provides quick sugar.

Nuts, seeds, and bars offer balanced energy.

Energy gels and chews are optional.

Chocolate melts. Jerky attracts wildlife and lingers in gear.

Bought Meals

"Never ride past food"

Even after eating, stop again if opportunity arises. It protects onboard supplies and improves morale. Conversations with locals often provide valuable route insight.

Hygiene

Cleanliness on a long ride is less about comfort and more about health.

A small toiletry kit is sufficient: toothbrush, tiny toothpaste, biodegradable soap, a small microfibre towel, and a minimal first-aid pouch.

Wet wipes can restore morale when water is scarce, but pack them out. A small bottle bidet attachment weighs little and improves hygiene significantly.

Chamois care is critical if you ride in padded shorts. Wash and dry properly whenever possible. Saddle sores can end a trip faster than mechanical failures.

Toilet

OK, it's time to deal with this subject. Having a bowel movement out in the wilderness isn't everyone's idea of quality time in nature.

You do need to think it through. I've heard many stories of novices who have managed to drop their first bowel movement straight into their riding shorts - not a great way to start the day.

To keep this short and practical: pick a spot where you'll feel comfortable. Take something to clean yourself afterwards (wet wipes are generally easier than toilet paper). De-robe in a way that makes it unlikely you'll get any poo (or wee) on yourself, squat down, and do what you need to do.

Simple.

If you have biodegradable wet wipes and the ground permits, dig a small hole and bury them. Otherwise, you'll need to pack them out with you. I normally carry a stash of sandwich bags to keep things dry and separate - they're a good way to store used wipes until you find a bin.

Navigation

Modern navigation is excellent - but it should never be singular.

A dedicated GPS bike computer is efficient and weather resistant. Many riders use platforms like Komoot or Ride with GPS to build routes.

Smartphones are powerful backup tools, but they are vulnerable to rain, damage, and battery drain.

Paper maps remain underrated. They provide strategic overview and never run out of power.

Before departure, download offline maps. In remote regions, assume no signal.

Power Systems

Everything now requires charging: GPS, phone, lights, headlamp.

A high-capacity power bank (10,000–20,000 mAh) is usually sufficient for several days. Fast-charging capability reduces time spent in cafés guarding wall sockets. Note: airlines only usually permit up to 10,000 mAh devices.

Dynamo hubs offer near self-sufficiency. They add cost and minor drag but provide consistent power during movement above 10kmh.

A4 sized ultralight solar panels are also an option, use them to charge the power bank not individual devices, especially your phone. Charge devices from the power bank at night.

Cables fail more often than devices. Carry one spare.

Recharge whenever possible - even if devices are not empty.

Lights

Cycling on trails in daylight hours means that for most of the time, you don't need lights. When you find yourself on sections of road, or you have early starts / late finishes – then they become essential. I look for front lights with long burn times on the lowest (usually ~250 lumens) setting rather than massive lumens capability. Blasting the countryside and other road users with 1000 lumens brings little benefit and quickly reduces the burn time.

A head torch is also extremely valuable, they are great for pitching tents late in the evening, cooking dinner, making sure you don't trip over if going for a midnight wee, checking that you've packed up everything if starting early. They can also be a backup or additional front light if required.

New Bike?

I have a hunch this section will generate some reaction - from you and from anyone you share it with.

A lot of people considering bikepacking already have a target bike in mind and are looking for confirmation that it's the right choice. Others already own a bike and want reassurance that they made the correct decision.

The unfortunate truth? There is no single perfect bike or formula for bikepacking.

Even if there were, it would likely be surpassed by something new very quickly - and contradicted by someone else's opinion in any case.

Fear not. There is a way to narrow down what your next bike should be.

Over the last few years, some trends have emerged. There are common tactics, and there are choices that are highly individual.

So, back to the beginning: there may not be a perfect bike, but there are ways to get into the right ballpark. The rest depends on you - your ability, your destination, and how long you're going for.

Let's start from the ground up.

Tyres ("Rubber")

Choose a tyre width that hits your sweet spot between speed, comfort, and safety. For me, that's usually 2.6" (66mm) tubeless Mezcals.

If you're confident on loose terrain and want to maximise daily kilometres, you can go as narrow as you dare.

That said, you don't see many riders using less than 1.77" (45mm). Smaller tyres are lighter but require higher pressures, which reduces comfort and tends to increase punctures - often for minimal speed gains.

If you're racing and willing to accept extra discomfort and risk, go narrow.

If you're riding long distances, value comfort, and want fewer repairs, go wider.

Tubes vs Tubeless

This often depends on where you're riding.

In remote or underdeveloped regions, tubes may be the safer choice - finding tubeless tyres or repair supplies can be difficult.

In most developed countries, I recommend tubeless. On a recent ride, a bike shop found six cactus spikes and a small nail in my rear tyre - I had no idea. That's the beauty of tubeless systems with quality sealant.

They're also slightly lighter.

Still, carry a spare tube for catastrophic punctures that won't seal or can't be plugged. More on that in the spares section.

Wheels

The two main considerations: material and spoke count.

Once a carbon rim cracks, it's game over.

An alloy rim can often be repaired well enough to keep riding.

So, for remote expeditions: alloy.

Near civilisation: carbon is fine, though not essential.

Bikepacking rigs get heavy - especially in dry climates where you carry extra water. A 24-spoke wheel can be under significant strain. The weight penalty of 36 spokes is minimal.

If in doubt, go with 36 spokes - especially on the rear wheel.

Frame

Material: Steel, Carbon, or Titanium

Steel:

Often overlooked as "old school," but a quality steel frame rides beautifully and can sometimes be bent back into shape after damage. The downside is weight.

Carbon:

Light and responsive. But more vulnerable to impact damage and transmits more high-frequency vibration, which can fatigue hands and arms on long rides.

Titanium:

Strong, relatively light, corrosion-resistant - and expensive. It's a superb compromise, though not the lightest or the most repairable.

Geometry

Geometry is arguably more important than material.

Mountain bike-style geometry (longer wheelbase, slacker head angle) is becoming more common in bikepacking. It handles technical terrain better and allows for dropper posts and suspension.

The trade-off? A smaller front triangle, limiting frame bag capacity.

Gravel-style geometry resembles a road bike but allows wider tyres and broader gearing. Faster on smoother surfaces; less forgiving off-road.

Your target terrain types should dictate your choice.

Forks

Traditionally, bikepacking bikes run rigid forks with mounting points for cages or panniers.

Arguments against suspension:

- Added weight
- Fewer mounting options
- More maintenance risk

Arguments for suspension:

- Dramatically improved comfort
- Better control on rough terrain

If you're prioritising speed and simplicity: rigid.

If comfort and technical terrain matter: consider suspension.

There are middle-ground options, such as suspension stems combined with wider, lower-pressure tyres.

Be cautious with certain lightweight suspension fork designs (e.g. Lauf) if loading the front heavily - frame wobble can be amplified at speed and across rocky terrain.

Drivetrain

This includes everything from pedals to rear axle: cranks, bottom bracket, chainring, chain (or belt), derailleur, cassette.

Traditional Derailleur Setup

Common, widely supported, and lighter. Gravel and MTB setups differ mainly in cassette range and chainring size.

Gravel: e.g. 10–40 cassette, ~40T chainring

MTB: e.g. 10–52 cassette, ~32–34T chainring

Larger cassette range = easier climbing.

Smaller chainring = easier climbing.

Unless racing, climbing ability usually matters more than top speed. Walking every hill isn't fun.

Gearbox / Internal Systems

Gearboxes (e.g. bottom bracket-integrated systems) house gears internally, making them highly durable.

Upsides:
Extremely dependable
Low maintenance

Downsides:
Special frame required
Added cost and weight

Rear hub systems (like Rohloff-style hubs) offer similar benefits without needing a dedicated frame - though you'll need a specific rear wheel.

Both systems can run with chain or belt drive. Belt drives reduce maintenance to almost zero but require a frame that allows belt installation.

Handlebars

Two main types: drop or flat.

Flat bars:
Greater control
More mounting space
Better leverage

Drop bars:
Multiple hand positions
More aerodynamic
Reduced mounting space

For long days, multiple hand positions can be invaluable.

Material matters too.

Carbon: lighter, but vulnerable in crashes - and bikepacking bikes fall over more than you think.

Aluminium: slightly heavier, more durable in rough use.

Saddle

This is critical - and highly individual.

Some riders swear by leather saddles. Others hate them.

There's no formula. Trial and error is usually the only way to find your perfect saddle.

Don't underestimate this. After a few days on the wrong saddle, you'll want to quit.

More trips end early due to saddle discomfort than almost anything else.

Bags

Expect your setup (excluding food and water) to add at least 5kg. Most riders carry 7–11kg. Some carry much more.

Volume matters as much as weight - cold-weather gear quickly fills space.

Bag Types (Front to Back)

Front panniers: Low weight distribution but can affect steering.

Handlebar roll: Ideal for light, bulky items (sleeping bag).

Snack/feed bags: Easy one-hand access.

Top tube bag: Electronics, snacks, tools.

Frame bag: Best place for heavy items (low centre of gravity).

Rear saddle bag: High but versatile; can affect balance.

Rear rack bag: Stable platform; slightly heavier system.

Rear panniers: Stable and low but encourage overpacking.

A "classic" bikepacking setup often includes:

Front roll
Frame or top tube bag
Large saddle bag

Once you add multiple panniers, you edge toward touring territory - not wrong, just different.

Brakes

Get the best you can.

Disc brakes are essential. Rim brakes are inadequate for heavy loads, steep gradients, and wet conditions.

Remember: braking systems are typically designed around a lighter rider on a light bike. A loaded bikepacking rig may add 20kg or more.

That extra mass puts serious demand on your brakes - especially on long twisty descents.

Dropper Post

I didn't use one for years - now I wish I had.

They dramatically improve control and confidence on descents.

However, oversized saddle bags can interfere with dropper function. You may need to manually pull it up - which can introduce instability.

One solution is switching to a rack system, lowering weight and freeing the dropper - at the cost of added weight.

CHAPTER 18

The Distance Between Your Ears

The Mental Edge of Bikepacking

Physical fatigue is predictable.

Mental fatigue is what ends many trips.

There will be moments when:

- 🚲 The headwind feels personal
- 🚲 The climb feels endless
- 🚲 The map feels intimidating
- 🚲 The rain feels unfair

This is normal.

The riders who continue are not the strongest.
They are the most mentally adaptable.

This chapter will go deeper into your mindset, like the previous chapter that went deeper into your equipment.

The Three Mental Phases of Every Tough Day

Phase 1: Resistance

"This is harder than I thought."

Phase 2: Negotiation

"Maybe I should stop. Maybe I can't."

Phase 3: Breakthrough

"I'm still moving."

The breakthrough rarely feels dramatic. It feels quiet. Steady. Calm.

You realise you are still pedalling.

And that is enough.

Micro-Goals Win Big Days

When a climb feels impossible, don't think about the summit.

Think:

- 🚲 To that tree.
- 🚲 To that bend.
- 🚲 Ten more pedal strokes.

Progress shrinks problems.

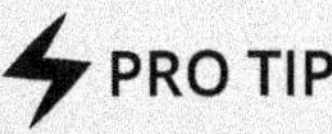 **PRO TIP**

Never make big decisions at your lowest energy point.

Eat. Drink. Rest. Then reassess.

 *Real-World Example*

On a steep mountain pass late in the day, a rider considered quitting the route entirely. Instead, they stopped, ate, waited 15 minutes, and continued slowly. That pass became their proudest memory of the trip.

Energy shifts change perspective.

The Power of Self-Talk

Replace:
"I can't do this."

With:
"I'm doing this slowly."

Language shapes endurance.

Why the Hard Days Matter

Comfort builds skill.
Difficulty builds identity.

The hard days are the ones you remember.

The Three Rollercoasters

Every adventure has its ups and downs - the climbs you can see, and the ones you carry inside your own head.

There are three rollercoasters. They are always running.

Rollercoaster 1 – The End-to-End Adventure

It begins with an idea.

Then comes the planning.

Telling family and friends.

The training.

The preparation.

And finally - the moment you commit and roll onto the trail.

This first rollercoaster will test you before you even begin. It will whisper doubts. It will ask whether you are ready. Whether this is sensible. Whether this is you.

Remember:

Preparation removes unwanted surprises.

Training hardens your body.

Practice builds experience.

Experience builds confidence.

Confidence carries you to the finish line.

Rollercoaster 2 – The Riding Day

You wake up re-energised. Ready. Focused.

Then the day unfolds.

The weather shifts.

A mechanical issue appears.

Your calf tightens.

Small problems line up, waiting to steal momentum.

This is where many riders lose the day.

So pause. Take a breath. Think clearly.

Explore your options.

There is no prize for rushing a poor decision. Get off the bike. Reset. Regain control. Solutions appear when panic disappears.

Stay calm. Stay deliberate. Stay moving.

Rollercoaster 3 – Hour to Hour

This one is the most unpredictable.

One minute you feel ten feet tall and unstoppable.

The next, you question every decision you have ever made.

Energy rises. Energy crashes.

Belief surges. Belief fades.

When it dips: Drink some water, eat a snack.

Focus on the next small win.

Not the summit. Not the finish. The next corner. The next climb. The next five minutes.

Momentum is rebuilt in inches.

These three rollercoasters are always in motion. And because they run at different rhythms, there will be rare, electric moments when you crest all three at once.

Those are the days you will talk about for the rest of your life.

These moments, the moments when everything is in your favour are truly the 'Magic Miles'. Savour them, bask in them.

But there will also be days when you hit the bottom of all three at the same time.

That is where character is forged.

That is where resolve becomes real.

You are not here by accident. To reach this point, you have already proven you are capable. When the low point arrives, acknowledge it. Own it. Endure it.

Because it will pass.

Keep the pedals moving.

And soon enough, the climb begins again.

What stories you are building!

CHAPTER 19

The Community and Culture of Bikepacking

Even when riding solo, you are part of something larger.

Bikepacking culture is built on things like:

- 🚴 Shared knowledge
- 🚴 Route recommendations
- 🚴 Honest gear discussions
- 🚴 Encouragement

It is one of the most welcoming outdoor communities in the world.

The Trail Code

Unspoken rules:

- 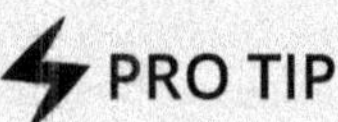 Share water information
- Help with repairs
- Respect campsites
- Encourage beginners

Your behaviour shapes the culture.

Events and Gatherings

Bikepacking events are not races in the traditional sense. They are shared challenges.

You'll find:

- Support
- Stories
- Connection

And often lifelong friendships.

⚡ **PRO TIP**

Say yes to at least one community event.

Growth accelerates around other motivated riders.

 *Tales from the trails...*

It's easy to think of bikepacking as a solitary pursuit - rider, bike, horizon. But again and again, I've been reminded that the journey is rarely just about the people pedalling.

In one single week, I experienced more unexpected generosity than I could reasonably explain.

High on a remote mountain trail - the kind where you start narrating your own documentary because you haven't seen another human in two days - I rounded a corner and nearly rode straight into a gazebo. Yes, a gazebo.

Under it stood a couple in their sixties who had somehow coaxed a 4x4 up the mountain pass. A gas BBQ was sizzling. Deck chairs were neatly arranged like a wilderness café.

"Are you okay?" the lady called cheerfully.

"Yes...?" I replied, unsure if altitude had finally got to me.

"Oh good. We're just cooking elk burgers from our farm for any riders coming through today."

They sat me down, handed me hot coffee, served an elk burger exactly as advertised, and finished with an oversized homemade cookie. A few hours later I was still riding in stunned silence.

The next day, a battered truck crawled toward me across a now flat desert track. The driver rolled down his window and, without ceremony, handed me two perfectly ripe oranges. No speech. Just kindness.

Later on that week, on a long road section with 100km still to town, another truck pulled over. The driver hopped out, opened a cooler, and produced ice-cold bottles of water. It was blisteringly hot. He'd had a hunch riders might be out there, so he'd packed ice and gone looking.

There are days on the bike when the wind feels endless and the climbs feel personal.

And then there are moments like these - small, generous, human moments - that quietly restore your faith in the world.

You start the ride for the landscape.

But often, it's the people who stay with you.

CHAPTER 20

The Responsibility of the Rider

Adventure without responsibility often ends in damage.

Bikepackers travel through fragile landscapes.

Your tyre tracks should be temporary.
Your impact should be minimal.

Core Environmental Principles

- Pack out all waste
- Avoid damaging trails in wet conditions
- Respect wildlife
- Use established campsites where possible

Why Stewardship Matters

Access depends on behaviour.

If riders damage landscapes, routes close.

If riders protect landscapes, routes expand.

You are not just a rider.
You are a representative.

⚡ PRO TIP

If unsure whether your action harms the environment - choose the more conservative option.

The Bigger Picture

Bikepacking deepens connection to land.

When you sleep under stars and cross remote valleys under your own power, you understand what is worth protecting.

Make this protection personal.

CHAPTER 21

The Rider You Become

At the beginning of this book, we talked about independence.

Now let's talk about identity.

Somewhere between your first overnight trip and your longer adventures, something shifts.

You stop asking:
"Can I do this?"

You start thinking:
"Where next?"

That shift is powerful.

Bikepacking Teaches You:

- How to prepare
- How to adapt
- How to endure
- How to solve problems
- How to stay calm under pressure

These skills do not disappear when the trip ends.

They follow you home.

The Hidden Transformation

You learn that discomfort is temporary.

You learn that problems are solvable.

You learn that forward progress, however slow, changes outcomes.

And most importantly, you learn that you are capable of more than you assumed.

Real-World Reflection

Ask any experienced bikepacker about their favourite trip.

They rarely mention speed.

They rarely mention gear.

They mention moments:

- 🚲 Sunrise over ridgelines
- 🚲 Quiet gravel roads
- 🚲 Shared meals
- 🚲 Unexpected kindness
- 🚲 Finishing something that felt intimidating

Those are identity moments.

You Don't Need Permission

You also do not need:

- 🚲 Perfect fitness
- 🚲 Perfect gear
- 🚲 Perfect timing

You need preparation.
You need respect.
You need willingness.

That's it.

The Invitation

Start small.

Plan well.

Pack intelligently.

Ride steadily.

Adapt calmly.

And keep going.

There are landscapes waiting for you.

There are skills waiting to grow.

There is confidence waiting to be built.

And there is a version of you - stronger, calmer, more capable - that only appears when you decide to pedal into the unknown.

So...

Bikepacking is not about escaping life.

It is about expanding it.

Now you have the knowledge.

Now you have the systems.

Now you understand the risks and the rewards.

It is time for you to start collecting your own "Tales from the trails"

The only question left is simple:

When do you start?

About the Author

For most of my school years, I rode a bicycle out of necessity. It was simply how I got from one place to another. I never imagined that decades later, that same simple machine would become one of the most meaningful parts of my life.

At 45, I returned to cycling, initially just to stay fit and clear my head. I wasn't chasing records or recognition - just movement, fresh air, and a sense of wellbeing. But somewhere along the way, short rides became long ones, and long ones became journeys.

Bikepacking gave my cycling direction. It offered goals to work toward, horizons to follow, and quiet challenges that reshaped how I saw myself.

Over the past ten years, I've been fortunate to cycle more than 66,000 kilometres across eight countries. Each journey has been a lesson in patience and perspective. From Osaka to Hiroshima in Japan, Seoul to Busan in South Korea, and through the diverse landscapes of Thailand, I learned to embrace both discomfort and wonder. I pedalled the length of New Zealand on the Tour Aotearoa, crossed parts of Australia from Sydney to Surfers Paradise and Melbourne to Canberra, and took on the epic Great Divide Mountain Bike Route through the USA and Canadian Rocky Mountains.

These rides aren't achievements I claim as trophies, but milestones that remind me what steady effort can accomplish. Cycling has taught me that progress is rarely dramatic - it's built one quiet, consistent turn of the pedals at a time.

Acknowledgements

My bikepacking brains trust and cycling crew:

Steve Church

Rob Hughes

Jon Dibbs

Greg Watt

Brian Payne

Adam Bentley

David 'The Big Cheese' Thomson

Steve & Kami Dibden

Inspiration for the Mantra & Magic Miles

Stephen Legate